FINISHING LINE PRESS
www.finishinglinepress.com

In Our Now

poems by

Valyntina Grenier

Finishing Line Press
Georgetown, Kentucky

In Our Now

dedicated to Camille Moitoret for giving me a copy of
The Botany of Desire *and to Michael Pollan for writing it.*

ISBN 978-1-64662-944-2 First Edition

ACKNOWLEDGMENTS

Thank you to the following presses and journals for publishing poems from this collection:

Fever Dream/ Take Heart, Cathexis Northwest Press, 2020.
The Impossible Beast: Poems of Queer Eroticism, Damaged Goods Press, 2020.
Beyond Words Magazine
Cathexis Northwest Press
High Shelf Press
The Night Heron Barks
Not Your Mother's Breast Milk
The Wardrobe
Wild Roof Journal

Publisher: Leah Huete de Maines
Editor: Christen Kincaid
Cover Art: Valyntina Grenier and Joseph Mark Hanson courtesy of Billie Bixby
Author Photo: Valyntina Grenier
Cover Design: Elizabeth Maines McCleavy

Order online: www.finishinglinepress.com
also available on amazon.com

Author inquiries and mail orders:
Finishing Line Press
PO Box 1626
Georgetown, Kentucky 40324
USA

Table of Contents

I selected the initial lexicon for these poems from Michael Pollan's *The Botany of Desire.* I chose, one to three consecutive words from a page or pages of Pollan's prose for the first draft of my poem. I dictated the selected text into notes on my iPhone. Voice recognition added some surprising turns when it misheard. I used the block of recorded text like a puzzle. I favored sound over sense. Meaning, more vocabulary, cuts, line breaks, stanzas, and transpositions followed.

IN OUR NOW

ordinary vision
is a hinge
crowded with flowers

busy/ multifarious
It feels like a city
In a quiet corner

a confusion of color and scent
is set to a railroad of insects
A carnelian dragonfly hovers to rest

after taking a turn on
our eye
Our eye?

All of the potential pollinators
Old roses leave behind
waded tissue

Inebriated anemones
are dining and humping
Trashed lilies lean in

Accept the invitation
into their throats of nectar
Afterward punch the air

IMPORTANT CLASSES

Fruit, flower and drug staple time
or another intimate stories each chapter
starts out
stops by

ventures far afield
for a brief perverse moment of
precious gold

Corporate engineers are reinventing love
People are nature telling ourselves what we call time has glazed
 across the galaxies
or a pathetic fallacy

It's a shame
even when the tenor changes
the gulf remains

An old "heroic" man emerges
Precious history paddles a canoe

Environmental morality
pays for transgressions
usually in coin

Disasters can't shake
how different aims
wrap us in the reciprocal web of

hope clothes us
From covers we'll look up
a little road

won't appear so alien and intimate
Design and desire

our knees and genius
recklessly remarkably
unself-conscious at the mirror

TRY THE GOAT

Amazon takes our minds off the forest the rain the taste
on the tongue rendering the most floral fruit putrid by design
Cattle with consequences like tweakers grind

Hallucinogenic like when seagull suggests adventurous Virgil's
    garden
as a source eddies on the wind
goats will try any angle

Increments do interesting things to animals
Arise toxify the goat *Minimize*
dangerous sustainable quantities of heightened powers humans allow
    to prove fatal

to figure somehow a single/ safe/ forbidden counterstrategy
animals intoxicate deliberately commonly
the sun eats its chromosomes explodes compounds mutates
    ultraviolet light prevents

    a caterpillar that leaves growing into butter trial and error
Photo synthesizers present species w/ a wild phosphorescent burn
Some plant paralyzer convulsive

and just caffeine unhinged w/ in
a nervous system kill-drive
man-man predators stuffing their brains with visions to enslave our
    world

That time the same abominable mystery that dazzling arts
brought even darker warfare
    poisons the vast chemical horrors atomized in protest

CITY'S LIMIT

Wade out with the uprising before long police
will come with canisters of gas *kill the lights* shattered glass
Maybe too much mayhem w/ looting at a few sites
Family businesses burning

We make disasters
Storms and droughts remind me how
imperfect human power whose pristine rose really is a freak more
powerful than corruption/ copulation/ Covid is

Capitalism atomizes
plants/ police kill
black people/ they/ women/ children/ men
their perfect geometry savagely lynched

proof of true evil
A single still image of
one wracked too scared person too ruined to withstand fury and
disregard
White superiority governs power

my white silence
white privilege
White fear
our forty-fifth president who cares

for his own mortality tweets
desires order on parade
to be photographed flanked
by armed men

Our racist-gun-toting-limited-confidence/ good/ sense
Karens threaten/ feel threatened/ report
a bump in a superstore or birdwatching in Central Park
People see nature's peaceful stirring as a riot of spring cities

love off rhythm
free green ground
our new centuries-old loam
People found a garden before plagues

before rampancy/ pharmacies before enslaved
people cleared and sewed
OK legions of poets chant a word
The illusion/ rendition of ordered earth I'd call an oxymoron
probably is

Experience femeral nature make her way with our before power
feeling
Small talk about opposite dubious beholding
labor and intelligence
our mortal earth the same Niagara or Everest impulse w/ which
farmers rose-stitched Versailles

Excite/ fill us
with a sense of our equanimous power
a kind location
both literal and moral

a violent-word-wilderness by comparison to our desire to exert
control
Wildness bristles w/ ambiguity and sure power
The farmer and the gardener understand power
affection on lock beyond suspension of disbelief

Protest
Harvest/ raze/ torch
the garden
Plant again

HELP A HUNDRED BILLION HONEYBEES POWDER THEIR THIGHS

Fact is we've been aware of indifference to the flower taking part in every being

As acorns witness somewhat self-centered angiosperms move freely trial and error find the best way to induce mater *by playing*

Or flowers manage to choose the exact moment seduced
off its knobby charms

Clever purposeful fungus conceives
of rotting meat

We care about making copies
Cost and taste make us mortals risk covid for a burger and fries

Time and location select countless generations
Design and catenation are culled by miracle

Trivial semiconscious evolution insists
as this novel strain mounts deaths

a token inventing/ insider/ outlaw contingent desires apparel and impunity

PRESSED AGAINST THIS SMART GLASS

Happen to find yourself a particular afternoon notice a makeshift
craft
floating through the narrow and bounded by steep shoulders
waterway

Notice fairies harnessed/ boiled a ramshackle armada of miracles
from the comparative wilderness caught that afternoon
care evidently distrusting the order 'wanted alive'

Hollowed out logs lashed to a skinny man w/ a burlap sack deemed
to be snoozing
A rent in the net under the weight of streams blanketed with moss

The sun already knows my nickname
An arrow shot clean through my ribs
Clock fragmented clots of day

plan/ plant/ drain the fertile forest hills
The wilderness riding me
out across out of print autobiography

w/ a resonance of mathematics learned bargaining sharply
for apples can tease murderers and settlers to domesticate the frontier
with old world exotics

Disparagement might return a golden habitat
an emblem of marriage
from man's peculiar craft

Passengers point at a sign
working for food
waiting for the bumblebee to wake up to hover among wide eyed

We give credit the power domestication represents
take to dance
Generations assume naive scenes
Animals sit it out

Nutritious acorns buried any arrangement with us long before
boatloads dependent on bank territory or at least the folk hero
  I figured

Modest our orchard or/
our childlike wishful/ wistful thinking
how lost

We accept fate in the tang of strangeness sweetened beyond
  recognition
a blemish free plastic dimension
one all-purpose-single-use-just-as-described-cheap-fake-sugar-
  substitute for the strong desire to
  live to

lounge in queerness
with no address
Hallow defiance
a night swim

a vegan frontier
do you mind
to ride a horse or punish a worm

Children are not rumors

For some cis-godfearing-rapist-white-men emphasis relies on their
  dress/
color of skin/ mitigation/ migration/ maps

Some far flung account/ song led to the river
the reality and the pipe littered behind

FOR THE LEAST DEAD BRAINS

These synthesize molecules

These design brains

Animals sometimes attract a flower
So a hummingbird slips her tender tongue from her hovering needle-like bill

But often animals repel
even destroy outright

flowers/ poisons
lick frogs' viscous skin

Here—one species of hairy prick because a powerful-death-dealing-selective-predator eyes
the great evolution of pesticides

Designed to kill is rendered better to repel/ confound/ cancerous facts
to expand the astounding

earning potential

ARE GRAMMAR'S ACTIVE SUBJECTS PASSIVE OBJECT'S EVERY SENSE?

As grasses conquer trees
origin demonstrates an outlandish new theory
artificial selection/ domesticated artifact/ a fake hybrid rose
is nature determining new forms and rules

deciding how wellness will be passed
w/ special injections
A tiny pharmaceutical force felt the world round
Modification by resignation storms our reflection

Great has come to mean
absurdity rules space
Call the wild innocent influence to blow wilderness
planting trees the wild's last default

Nature cum wiki-civilization
Look apples/ pandas/ ocelots
ozone holes pass
futures strangely uncharted

Take place
a set of ever-expanding characters plants a world
Woven lives we clearly suspect
default under civilization's white house

The metaphor is somehow
something happens outside simply
imagination's nature is also in
the kitchen

the brain
the holding up to look
inhaling smoke
the sway and the swagger

THE PLANT'S EYE

This is speculation I know but
idol flowers have always born
our mean-making scissors

Consider scissors nature's trope
deploying astonishing devices

The pitcher
marooned and white
not attractive unless

you reinforce the species
w/ a question of mimicry
intended to scare Victorians

An arc of corseted breasts
crowned w/ clitoria

Consider an insect
evolved to conceive
as female and male

captivatingly from behind
A frenzy of intercourse

ensures pollination
Our factory is olfactory
tactile attention not just to

simple chemicals
signals so far as creatures are things
to secure pollination or a meal

It's in our sanctum
Call the behavior
pseudo-copulation

Call the flower sex-worker
As bees rush around mounting

disseminating genes
flowers traffic metaphor

a meadow brims
with our making
Move the garden

Multiply
Flowers take aim

Secure/ obscure notions from long ago
crossed our own offspring

That match the
symbiosis of desire
in the garden on fire

AT THE FRONT OF THE PERENNIAL BED

At the front of the perineal bed there's a low soft forest of spikes

Look—dipped into that vibrating cloud's hairy irresistible bees
swimming with male and female genitalia

the floral point
They avoid pollinating themselves

Self-pollination is overdue
w/ a stamen and pistol to stagger the times

Receptive among them sweets extend
with slender admittance to their first prying open

Pursed lips coil

Bees' desire is grafted in architecture
as the around us is surrounded in honeycomb

Hear the bees leeward
nosing like pigs through golden dust

rolling tenderly in a purple medusa
Transports of ecstasy are a projection

a magic beyond flower bee embrace
a designer drug deployed to drive lost work

Fine penises and prostitutes
deem themselves sugary nectars

I've fixed on the bee's eye

The perspective of the human looms
crowds with our species of harms

All the sacrificed ones wish
grander and probably designed

ideals of tenderness
didn't go unrecognized

In the cell where the eye is
lilies lend their faces

their favor shores
salacious pubic blame

I CALLED BOTANY AS MUCH ABOUT THE HUMMINGBIRDS' LOVE

I called botany as much about the hummingbirds' love
as a human equivalent

Poor history
leaving altered notions through tanning

Intoxication
specifically ancient arts headed toward the gravitational pull
usher beauty into the moment

Attraction by token has a handful of chemicals
pleasure/ money/ a wormhole
that tubers, docile rams and
strangers mark

A marvelous imagination of aims
sheers some pardon history plays
Complexity and sophistication perfect how to refine our abilities' ore
so we are told

Making language our alchemist
transforms sunlight into accomplished beings
to manufacture

Nailing the astonishing trick
physics poisons
and delights

Rows and sheep power dreams
Trouble plants in our brains

to devise divisive recipes
Deadly poisons confect pedicures

Stirring in gratifying fact
mobility can't move/ locomote/ pray on

our tangled sleep
Strange

A GREAT HELP

All the people give time and knowledge

Privilege and pleasure imagine trust

Errors remain heartfelt

Patience, humor and love
are our seeds
selling pleasant odes

Plenty of vibrating bees
X a stench of human beings

We should be riding
indispensable friendship

w/ an ear and eye
morphed of gratitude

We garden and stumble
spend a laughable afternoon
disseminating genes

species fingering
our sovereign prerogative

to thrive and charge
The long chain

engineers, breeders, days
choose/ call/ harvest/ divide

Wondering at a bum plundering for nectar
is a self-serving conceit

in genes consciousness means

PLEASANT DESULTORY WORK

May afternoon suddenly appear
in manifold delights
the tung oil so innocent
acting on me
getting me to polish

Looking beyond the work bench
a same upside down book attempts
the story Human desires link destiny

Unconventional domestication
is something we do
something certain animals have done
Success surprises
the seahorse and the frog

We figure how to heal, clothe, intoxicate and otherwise elate
As some ancestor mastered our wild prized
wolves/ selves/ elves values fold
a sophisticated genome

We learn a great trick
ordinary credit
true volumes of ingenious sets
turn people into bees

Rich archives of DNA like sabers change beauty the
toxic unprepossessing
business of
remaking us

Valyntina's work is queer, feminist and fed up with capitalism. She was educated at The University of California, Berkeley, and St. Mary's College, Moraga. Graduating with an MFA in poetry, she is mostly self-taught as a painter, installation, and Neon artist.

Her visual art advocates for protecting our planet and all our vulnerable mortals. Her poems protest the racial and gender inequality at work in our political systems. Whether their initial lexicon is derived from source text, written by hand or recorded in the moment, her poems shape their sense from sound to attend the tenderness and violence that mark our human natures.

You can hear, see or read about her recent work in *Fever Dream/ Take Heart* (Cathexis Northwest Press, 2020), T*he Impossible Beast: Queer Erotic Poems* (Damaged Goods Press, 2020), *Bat City Review, Beyond Words Magazine, Cathexis Northwest Press, Gaze, High Shelf Press, Impermanent Earth, The Journal, Lana Turner, The Night Heron Barks, Sunspot Literary Journal* and *Wild Roof Journal.* Find her at valyntinagrenier.com or Insta @valyntinagrenier.

www.ingramcontent.com/pod-product-compliance
Lightning Source LLC
LaVergne TN
LVHW041523070426
835507LV00012B/1787
9781646629442